C000097283

# *At the foot of the cross*

# At the foot of the cross

TONY KIDD

SCRIPTURE UNION

Scripture Union, 207–209 Queensway, Bletchley, MK2 2EB, England.

© Tony Kidd 1998

First published 1998, reprinted 1999

ISBN 1 85999 247 1

All rights reserved. No part of this publication may be reproduced,
stored in a retrieval system, or transmitted, in any form or by any
means, electronic, mechanical, photocopying, recording or otherwise,
without the prior permission of Scripture Union.

The right of Tony Kidd to be identified as author of this work has been
asserted by him in accordance with the Copyright, Designs and Patents
Act 1988.

The Scripture quotations contained herein are from the New Revised
Standard Version Bible, copyright © 1989 by the Division of Christian
Education of the National Council of the Churches of Christ in the
USA, and are used by permission. All rights reserved.

British Library Cataloguing-in-Publication Data
A catalogue record for this book is available from the British Library.

Cover design by Mark Carpenter Design Consultants.
Illustrations by Brady Senior.

Printed and bound in Great Britain by Creative Print and Design Wales

# CONTENTS

# INTRODUCTION

Jesus carries the marks of the crucifixion into eternity, but the cross itself stays rooted in the soil of his prayers. What does it cost to pray for others despite our own suffering? Is it a price we are prepared to pay? Are we prepared to go to the place apart and face ourselves? The experience of those who went with Jesus to Gethsemane and to the foot of the cross challenges us to look at how we prepare for what may lie ahead.

This course has been written primarily for use by groups, although it may also be helpful to individuals. A group of six to ten people is ideal. Group members may want to appoint a leader, or take it in turns over the six weeks to be responsible for facilitating the group and keeping time. Allow between one-and-a-half and two hours for each session. Suggested timings for the specific sections are:

Way in .............10–15 minutes     Response ........15–20 minutes
Bible ...............20–30 minutes     Prayer .............10–20 minutes
Life ..................5–10 minutes

The songs for each session can be found in *Mission Praise* (MP), *Songs of Fellowship* (SOF) and *Let's Praise* (LP). There are also suggestions for music to be played when leading into times of prayer or during the meditations.

The meditations may be approached in three ways:

- You may like to read them on your own silently or, if no one else is near, out loud.

- If you are in a group, one person might read the meditation to the others. The passage should be read slowly, with pauses at appropriate points to allow time for people to take in the atmosphere and bring their imaginations into play.

- If the person reading to the group is feeling fairly confident, they might use the meditation as a basis for painting their own picture of the scene, pausing after each line to inject imagery or description.

An illustration appears near each meditation to provide a focus, but you may like to bring an appropriate object such as a spray of leaves or flowers, a cross or a candle. Other pictures, either photographs or prints of paintings, can be used. Be creative in thinking up ways to bring interest and variety to each session.

- At times of sharing, no one should feel obliged to say more than they want to, and individual privacy must always be respected. As a group, be sensitive to the possibility that some members may find parts of the sessions difficult. Providing support in such circumstances could be helpful.

- There are points in the sessions when silence can be used. Some may find silence uncomfortable, so offer reassurance beforehand. Let people know how long the silence will last, and that they can use it for quiet prayer, to unburden themselves from the pressures of the day, or simply to be still before God.

The pattern of prayer on pages 18–19 is designed for use each day during the course, and may be adapted to suit personal taste and practice. The daily readings form a natural part of the pattern of prayer. The following are the readings for the three days before the first meeting.

| Preparation | Day 1 | Numbers 21:4–9, The bronze serpent |
| --- | --- | --- |
| | Day 2 | 1 Kings 19:1–9, Food in the wilderness |
| | Day 3 | John 17:1–19, Jesus prays |
| **Meeting** | **Day 4** | **Matthew 26:36–46, Gethsemane** |

# *Session 1*
# **PRAYING IN GETHSEMANE**

## *Aim*
To look at the part that prayer plays in our response to life's hard times.

## *Way in*
Spend a few minutes talking to your neighbour about something that has cropped up recently (in the news, at home or at work) which you have found difficult and where prayer has been part of your response. Listen while your neighbour does the same. Using what you know, introduce your neighbour to the group.

### PREPARING
You may like to begin with some music to help you prepare to meet with God. For those who enjoy singing, the songs listed below reflect the theme of this first session. These are only suggestions: you may wish to choose your own.

### Songs to sing
'O Lord, hear my prayer', SOF 423, LP 149.
'Soften my heart, Lord', SOF 505, MP 606, LP 188.
'What a friend we have in Jesus', SOF 593, MP 746.
'I rest in God alone', MP 291, LP 79.
'Christ is the answer', MP 72.
'Do not be afraid', MP 115.
'Hear my cry, O God', MP 227.
'I look to the hills', MP 283.
'In thy presence', SOF 247.

**Music to listen to**
Handel: 'For behold, darkness shall cover the earth', 'The
    people that walked in darkness', from *Messiah*.
Paul McCartney: 'Meditation', from *Standing Stone*.

## Bible

**Matthew 26:36–46**
*36 Then Jesus went with them to a place called Gethsemane; and
he said to his disciples, 'Sit here while I go over there and pray.'
37 He took with him Peter and the two sons of Zebedee, and began
to be grieved and agitated. 38 Then he said to them, 'I am deeply
grieved, even to death; remain here, and stay awake with me.'
39 And going a little farther, he threw himself on the ground and
prayed, 'My Father, if it is possible, let this cup pass from me; yet
not what I want but what you want.' 40 Then he came to the disciples and found them sleeping; and he said to Peter, 'So, could you
not stay awake with me one hour? 41 Stay awake and pray that
you may not come into the time of trial; the spirit indeed is will-
ing, but the flesh is weak.' 42 Again he went away for the second
time and prayed, 'My Father, if this cannot pass unless I drink it,
your will be done.' 43 Again he came and found them sleeping, for
their eyes were heavy. 44 So leaving them again, he went away and
prayed for the third time, saying the same words. 45 Then he came
to the disciples and said to them, 'Are you still sleeping and tak-
ing your rest? See, the hour is at hand, and the Son of Man is
betrayed into the hands of sinners. 46 Get up, let us be going. See,
my betrayer is at hand.'*

In the garden of Gethsemane, Jesus, who is innocent of any
wrongdoing, faces up to a brutal and humiliating death. He
prays. His agony as he does so lies in the knowledge that he
must complete the task his Father has given him while over-
coming his natural, human feelings of abhorrence.

What we see as we look at the scene is someone encounter-
ing the most important decision of his life. Jesus is determined

to face up to the situation, but cannot avoid the distress that this naturally creates. While he is aware of the enormity of his mission, since earlier he had referred to all those who were affected by it (John 3:13–15), he cannot help the very human feelings he has.

The following meditation may help to give some sense of the crisis building up in the hours before Jesus' arrest.

## *Meditation*

### GETHSEMANE

It is a cool evening,
refreshing after the intense heat of the day.
We have left the city with its noises and smells
of feasting and food.
The path to Gethsemane seems so peaceful.
The sky is a great velvet curtain
dotted with gleaming silver stars,
some alone, some in huge clusters.
They seem so close, as if they were almost within reach.

The meal we just had together was different from others.
Jesus seemed reflective, almost sad.
Now we have come to this special place among the olives,
these huge trees, twisted by time.

Only eleven of us are with Jesus.
Judas has gone off by himself,
leaving before the meal was over.
Jesus is telling us to rest here,
but he wants James, Peter and John to go with him.

The four of them climb to a place where the ground is steeper,
the rocks larger and the trees more sparsely spread.
Jesus tells the three to stop and keep watch.
They don't know what he means,

but he seems so intense that none of them can ask.
Like the time they went with him to another high place.
Then he shone with light. But this is different.
He seems so sad,
so preoccupied and weighed down.

Jesus has moved on, but the three can still see him.
He lies down, with his face to the ground.
They can hear his voice, but not all the words.
He's agonising about a cup and doing his Father's will.
They have seen him pray before, but not like this.

It's warmer than they thought,
and they all wonder if ... wonder if...

Suddenly they wake up. Jesus stands before them.
He asks why they could not pray with him for just one hour.
They want to with all their hearts, but they are just so tired.
They promise to try again, and Jesus goes back to his place.
They see him praying so intensely
that the sweat gleams on his face in the moonlight.
All three begin praying hard ... praying hard ... praying...

Suddenly there's a lot of noise and lights.
A huge procession is entering the garden.
Jesus is telling us, shouting almost, to get up.
He says the hour has come.
There's Judas.
What on earth is going on?

**FOR DISCUSSION / REFLECTION**
Having imagined Jesus and the disciples in Gethsemane, what can
we learn from them about prayer in the face of adversity?

## Life
What makes matters worse for Jesus is knowing that he is about to
be condemned by those who profess to serve God, and betrayed by
one of his own disciples. Even his closest companions, Peter,

James and John, are unable to stay with him in prayer at this critical time.

Can you recall a situation where you either felt unjustly treated or let down by those on whom you thought you could rely?

*How did it feel?*                 *What did you think?*

*What did you do?*                 *Have you forgiven?*
                                   *Was this difficult?*

## Response

Without feeling that you have to disclose any of the detail of your experience, discuss with the group your response to the situation you encountered. How does remembering Jesus' experience help you come to terms with what happened to you?

## PRAYER

Use this time as an opportunity to share anything that has been particularly significant for you during this session, and pray about it together.

Further reflection on the theme of this session will be aided by using the readings for the week and the pattern of prayer outlined on pages 18–19. You may wish to do these, along with the words of praise and the meditation, as a group, or individually throughout the week.

## PRAISE

**Leader:** I will praise the Lord who counsels me.
**All:** Keep me safe, O Lord.
**Leader:** I have set the Lord always before me.
**All:** Keep me safe, O Lord.
**Leader:** My heart is glad and my tongue rejoices.
**All:** In you, O Lord, I take refuge.
**Leader:** You will fill me with joy in your presence.

*(Based on Psalm 16)*

# Meditation

## PRAYING IN GETHSEMANE

In this dark place of twisted shapes
what does obedience mean?
Do I follow the straight but painful path between the trees,
or hide in the tangled undergrowth of compromise?
It is so easy to find reasons not to act,
or to shelter behind arguments.
I can delay, ask for more time,
say I'm talking to others, pretend I haven't heard,
but then where is my faith?
Has it joined all the other 'Why nots?'
in the graveyard of integrity?
In the silence of Gethsemane waits the God
who listens for my response.

## Readings for the week

### 1 Praying in Gethsemane

| Reflection | Day 5 | Acts 7:54–60, Stephen prays |
| --- | --- | --- |
| | Day 6 | Romans 12:9–21, Faithful in prayer |
| | Day 7 | James 5:7–16, Patience in suffering |

### 2 A place apart

| Preparation | Day 1 | 1 Kings 8:1–26, In the temple |
| --- | --- | --- |
| | Day 2 | Jonah 2:1–10, In the belly of a great fish |
| | Day 3 | Mark 1:29–39, Jesus prays alone |
| **Meeting** | **Day 4** | **Matthew 6:5–15, The Lord's prayer** |

# *Pattern of prayer*

You may wish to use this pattern as a basis for your daily prayers during the course.

## PRAISE AND THANKSGIVING

Spend a few moments thinking of the things you want to thank God for, then offer them up to him in praise.

> I will praise you, O Lord, with all my heart;
> > I will sing praises to your name, O Most High.
> > > *(Based on Psalm 9:1-2)*

## CONFESSION

Spend a few moments thinking of things you need to confess, asking for forgiveness.

> Remember, O Lord, your great mercy and love;
> remember not the sins of my youth
> > and my rebellious ways;
> > according to your love, remember me.
> Look upon my affliction and my distress
> > and take away all my sins.
> > > *(Based on Psalm 25:6-7,18)*

> I said, 'I will confess my transgressions to the Lord',
> > and you forgave the guilt of my sin.
> > > *(Based on Psalm 32:5)*

## BIBLE

On each day when you are reflecting on the last session, re-read the key Bible passage for the session and make notes of any new thoughts or feelings you have.

*or*

On each day when you are preparing for the next session, read the Bible passage and spend time reflecting on it, making notes of any feelings you experience.

## *then*

Use the reading for the day, or the meditation for the week, to come and be still before God.

## INTERCESSION
Bring to God:
- any people or situations that you feel need his love
- the other members of the group
- your own needs

### The Lord's prayer
Our Father in heaven,
Hallowed be your name,
your kingdom come,
your will be done
on earth as it is in heaven.
Give us today our daily bread.
Forgive us our sins
as we forgive those who sin against us.
Lead us not into temptation
but deliver us from evil.
For the kingdom, the power and the glory are yours
    now and forever. Amen.

### In closing
Lord, let me go out in the peace of Jesus Christ.
    In his name I ask it. Amen.

# Session 2
# A PLACE APART

## Aim
To consider what is important about the place in which we pray.

## Way in
Discuss with another member of the group whether there is a particular place or set of circumstances which makes prayer easier for you.

### PREPARING
As before, you may like to begin with music. Then pray together about the things you have already talked about. Allow time for silent prayer and reflection.

### Songs to sing
'Be still and know', SOF 41, MP 48.
'Be still, for the presence of the Lord', SOF 40, MP 50, LP 13.
'Dear Lord and Father of mankind', SOF 79, MP 111.
'I heard the voice of Jesus say', SOF 215, MP 275.
'Just as I am', SOF 316, MP 396, LP 101.
'Living under the shadow of his wing', SOF 346, MP 423.
'The Lord's my shepherd', SOF 537, MP 660, LP 203(i).
'You are my hiding place', SOF 625, MP 793.
'Open our eyes, Lord', SOF 443, MP 545, LP 158.

### Music to listen to
Handel: 'He shall feed his flock like a shepherd', from *Messiah*.
Enya: 'Shepherd moons', from *Shepherd Moons*.

# Bible

## Matthew 6:5–15

*[Jesus said]* [5] *'And whenever you pray, do not be like the hypocrites;
for they love to stand and pray in the synagogues and at the street
corners, so that they may be seen by others. Truly I tell you, they
have received their reward.* [6] *But whenever you pray, go into your
room and shut the door and pray to your Father who is in secret; and
your Father who sees in secret will reward you.*

[7] *'When you are praying, do not heap up empty phrases as
the Gentiles do; for they think that they will be heard because of
their many words.* [8] *Do not be like them, for your Father knows
what you need before you ask him.*

[9] *'Pray then in this way:*
*Our Father in heaven,*
*hallowed be your name.*
[10] *Your kingdom come.*
*Your will be done,*
*on earth as it is in heaven.*
[11] *Give us this day our daily bread.*
[12] *And forgive us our debts,*
*as we have also forgiven our debtors.*
[13] *And do not bring us to the time of trial,*
*but rescue us from the evil one.*
[14] *For if you forgive others their trespasses, your heavenly Father
will also forgive you;* [15] *but if you do not forgive others, neither
will your Father forgive your trespasses.'*

The place for prayer may be anywhere we set aside or seek out
especially for that purpose. Jesus often left his disciples and the
crowds (eg Matt 14:13) and went to find a place apart, away
from other people, in order to pray. Even when he took Peter,
James and John (the disciples to whom he was closest) with him
in the garden of Gethsemane, Jesus left them in order to go apart
to pray alone.

Jesus prayed from the cross which was itself erected in a

place apart, outside the city wall. As on other occasions, those close to Jesus remained nearby but at a distance (Mark 15:40). The cross is a powerful symbol of exclusion. Jesus had to be like the sacrificial criminal, rejected and put out of the camp away from the people. We have to be prepared to go with him (Heb 13:12–13).

So there is an emphasis throughout Jesus' life on praying alone in a place apart, and this pattern has been followed down through the ages. Indeed, in times past, one of the features of Christian observance in wealthier homes was the *poustinia*. This was a small area, a cupboard or space walled off from the rest of the dwelling. It contained a chair, a small table, a candle, a Bible and a devotional object. There would be bread and some water and, on the wall opposite the chair, would be secured a cross.

For those not so well off, such as the parents of John and Charles Wesley, separate places for prayer and devotion were not possible. Thus it became established that if Mary Wesley, their mother, was observed with her apron over her head, she was at prayer and not to be disturbed.

## FOR DISCUSSION / REFLECTION

How practical is it in modern living accommodation to set aside a space for devotions (prayer, meditation, etc)? Is it something we should regard as an important objective? How can we overcome shortage of space?

How can we pray where circumstances are not ideal? In times of suffering, is praying in a place apart something that can help us? How important is praying with others during these times?

## Life

It may be very helpful to set aside a place apart for prayer and meditation. If we dedicate space to bathing or washing, why not space for praying? However, prayer also requires a space within ourselves which sees it as being important and gives it priority.

The purpose of the following exercise is to look at the space we occupy physically, and to examine the way in which we use the space inside ourselves.

## THE SPACE WE USE

### Physical

List the rooms in your home and their uses. What is the relative importance you attach to each room compared with the others? (Give a number between 1 and 5, where 5 is most important.)

| Room | Use | Importance |
|------|-----|------------|
|      |     |            |

Would a change in the way you use a space create a place apart for prayer? (For example, what use could be made of a room that is only occupied intermittently?)

## Spiritual

List the roles you have in your life, eg parent, employee, team leader. What is the relative importance you attach to each role compared with the others? (Give a number from 1–5 where 5 is most important.)

| *Roles* | *Importance* |
|---------|--------------|
|         |              |

Would a change in the way you spend your time create more space inside yourself for prayer? (Even giving prayer a little more emphasis may be helpful.)

## Response

As a group, discuss any ideas you may have on creating physical or personal space more prayerfully. Use this time as an opportunity to tell others in the group anything that has been particularly significant for you during the session.

Further reflection on the theme of this session will be aided by using the readings for the week and the pattern of prayer outlined on pages 18–19. You may wish to do these, along with the words of praise and the meditation, as a group, or individually throughout the week.

### PRAYER

People may wish to bring into the light of God's presence issues they feel need exploring further. Perhaps the Lord's prayer could be used as a basis on which to create your own prayers.

### PRAISE

**Leader:** The Lord makes me lie down in green pastures.
**All:** He is my shepherd.
**Leader:** He leads me beside still waters.
**All:** He is my shepherd.
**Leader:** He guides me in paths of righteousness.
**All:** I shall not want.
**Leader:** Though I walk through the valley of the shadow of death.
**All:** He is with me.
**Leader:** I will dwell in the house of the Lord for ever.

*(Based on Psalm 23)*

## Meditation

Deep within the secret place there stands a cross
which represents the life that Jesus offered up.
Its upright speaks of God's will done.
Across it are the arms that take in all the worldly wrongs
which otherwise would bar the way to paradise.
This crucifix, which occupies each heart, lies hidden,
but awaits the time when it may be discovered.

This happens when we come in prayer to offer up to God
the sins we acknowledge
and, repenting, start the journey Godwards.
Then we become empowered,
born again through the loving presence of the crucified.

## Readings for the week

**2 A place apart**

| Reflection | Day 5 | Acts 1:1–14, Common prayer |
|---|---|---|
| | Day 6 | Acts 10:9–23, Prayer on a roof |
| | Day 7 | Acts 16:13–15, Prayer by a river |

**3 Why have you forsaken me?**

| Preparation | Day 1 | Deut 31:14–22, Rebellion predicted |
|---|---|---|
| | Day 2 | Psalm 4, Singing in distress |
| | Day 3 | Micah 3, God's face is hidden |
| **Meeting** | **Day 4** | **Psalm 22, A prayer of anguish** |

# Session 3

# WHY HAVE YOU FORSAKEN ME?

## Aim

To reflect upon the times when we find ourselves in the 'wilderness', and our response to the experience.

## Way in

Make a note of the words or phrases that come into your mind when you think about the word 'forsaken'. Compare your list with that of another member of the group.

### PREPARING

Begin with a short period of silence (see page 8 for guidance on using silence). This time may be brought to a close with some suitable music.

### Music to listen to

Handel: 'He was despised', from *Messiah*.
Adiemus: 'Hymn', from *Songs of Sanctuary*.

## Bible

### Psalm 22:1–22

> *1 My God, my God, why have you forsaken me?*
> *Why are you so far from helping me, from the*
> *words of my groaning?*
> *2 O my God, I cry by day, but you do not answer;*
> *and by night, but find no rest.*

*3 Yet you are holy,*
*enthroned on the praises of Israel.*
*4 In you our ancestors trusted;*
*they trusted, and you delivered them.*
*5 To you they cried, and were saved;*
*in you they trusted, and were not put to shame.*

*6 But I am a worm, and not human;*
*scorned by others, and despised by the people.*
*7 All who see me mock at me;*
*they make mouths at me, they shake their heads;*
*8 'Commit your cause to the Lord; let him deliver –*
*let him rescue the one in whom he delights!'*

*9 Yet it was you who took me from the womb;*
*you kept me safe on my mother's breast.*
*10 On you I was cast from my birth,*
*and since my mother bore me you have been my God.*
*11 Do not be far from me,*
*for trouble is near*
*and there is no one to help.*

*12 Many bulls encircle me,*
*strong bulls of Bashan surround me;*
*13 they open wide their mouths at me,*
*like a ravening and roaring lion.*

*14 I am poured out like water,*
*and all my bones are out of joint;*
*my heart is like wax;*
*it is melted within my breast;*
*15 my mouth is dried up like a potsherd,*
*and my tongue sticks to my jaws;*
*you lay me in the dust of death.*

*16 For dogs are all around me;*
*a company of evildoers encircles me.*
*My hands and feet have shrivelled;*
*17 I can count all my bones.*

*They stare and gloat over me;*
*18 they divide my clothes among themselves,*
    *and for my clothing they cast lots.*

*19 But you, O Lord, do not be far away!*
    *O my help, come quickly to my aid!*
*20 Deliver my soul from the sword,*
    *my life from the power of the dog!*
        *21 Save me from the mouth of the lion!*

*From the horns of the wild oxen you have rescued me.*
*22 I will tell your name to my brothers and sisters;*
    *in the midst of the congregation I will praise you;*
*23 You who fear the Lord, praise him!*
        *All the offspring of Jacob, glorify him;*
        *stand in awe of him, all you offspring of Israel!*
*24 For he did not despise or abhor*
    *the affliction of the afflicted;*
*he did not hide his face from me,*
    *but heard when I cried to him.*

*25 From you comes my praise in the great congregation;*
    *my vows I will pay before those who fear him.*
*26 The poor shall eat and be satisfied;*
    *those who seek him shall praise the Lord.*
    *May your hearts live forever!*

*27 All the ends of the earth shall remember*
    *and turn to the Lord;*
*and all the families of the nations*
    *shall worship before him.*
*28 For dominion belongs to the Lord,*
    *and he rules over the nations.*

*29 To him, indeed, shall all who sleep in the earth bow*
            *down;*
    *before him shall bow all who go down to the dust,*
    *and I shall live for him.*
*30 Posterity will serve him;*

> *future generations will be told about the Lord,*
> *³¹ and proclaim his deliverance to a people yet unborn,*
> *saying that he has done it.*

In his final moments of agony on the cross, Jesus cried out, 'My God, my God, why have you forsaken me?' These words echo the opening of Psalm 22 which, with uncanny accuracy, describe what it might be like to undergo crucifixion. The words themselves ring out with the horror of the separation from God which Jesus, bearing the sins of the world, had to experience. Yet in this time of utter desolation, which he endured in obedience to his Father's will, Jesus overcame death when he surrendered his spirit to God.

The 'wilderness' times, when we feel separated from God, can come upon us for reasons which are all too obvious, or for no reason at all that we can see. Bereavement, loss of employment and the breakdown of relationships can all cause us to feel that God is absent. At least, in such circumstances, we can understand our feelings because we know the source. However, what if they arise from no discernible cause?

Job was, in God's eyes, a blameless and upright man, and yet enormous disasters befell him to such an extent that for him death became desirable (Job 3). Job's suffering, like that of Jesus after him, did not come about as the result of some personal misconduct. However, whereas Jesus accepted God's will in an act of complete surrender, Job had to be confronted by God before coming to terms with his situation (40:3–5; 42:1–6). And despite his desperate turmoil, Job foresees, by faith, the redemption Jesus would one day accomplish (16:9–21; 19:25–27).

The desert experience may come upon us unexpectedly, whether it be the result of a calamity we recognise as part of the natural process of life, or one whose cause we cannot understand. Then we may, like Job, be tempted to ask, 'Where have I gone wrong?' (6:24b).

## Life

Read Job's prayer (42:1–6). Spiritually, Job's eyes were opened when he came in faith to understand that God's plans for his life included suffering. Whereas Job's comforters presumed to know why disasters had befallen him, in reality they did not and were therefore guilty of spiritual arrogance.

Spend some time answering the following questions:

*Have you ever had feelings of remoteness from God or that he had let you down?*

*Were you tempted to blame God for this or to believe that he had deserted you?*

*If this has not been your experience, how have you
responded to others who have encountered these feelings?*

*Did you restore your relationship with God?
How did you do it? Did you find this difficult?*

*Was there anything you learned from the experience which
has helped you or other people subsequently?*

# Meditation

## SUFFERING

There are times when I look in upon the suffering of others
and I ask 'Why?'
Why him? Why like that? Why now?
More often than not there is, in response,
a silence large enough
to embrace me in its understanding.

Those who looked at Job – and later at Jesus –
asked the same questions.
And some, finding no answers,
turned aside and lost their way.
Those who remained learned that there is,
at the heart of it all,
One who suffers for creation,
who can understand and love us in our suffering.
It is part of what makes love the reason for being.

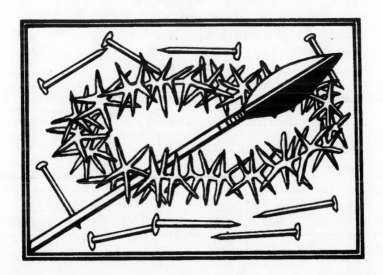

## *Response*

As a group, share one thing each that you have discovered during the Life section.

### PRAYER

People may wish to give thanks for the restoration of their relationship with God. Alternatively, it may be appropriate to pray for other significant things that have come to light during the session. Perhaps Jesus' prayer from the cross brings emotions of sorrow and thanksgiving to the surface. Allow people to express these feelings in their prayers. It may also be appropriate to use the meditation on page 35 at this point.

Further reflection on the theme of this session will be aided by using the readings for the week and the pattern of prayer outlined on pages 18–19. You may wish to do these, along with the words of praise and the meditation, as a group, or individually throughout the week.

### PRAISE

**Leader:** My soul thirsts for the living God.
**All:** Where can I go and meet with God?
**Leader:** Jesus has been my food day and night.
**All:** Where can I go and meet with God?
**Leader:** Why are you downcast, O my soul?
**All:** Put your hope in God.
**Leader:** I will praise him, my Saviour and my God.

*(Based on Psalm 42)*

## *Readings for the week*

**3 Why have you forsaken me?**

| Reflection | Day 5 | Ephesians 4:17–32, Living in the light |
| | Day 6 | Ephesians 5:8–21, Children of light |
| | Day 7 | Revelation 2:1–7, Do not fall away |

## 4 Father, forgive them

| Preparation | Day 1 | Genesis 50:15–21, Joseph forgives |
|---|---|---|
| | Day 2 | Matthew 18:21–35, The ungrateful servant |
| | Day 3 | Luke 7:36–50, The grateful woman |
| **Meeting** | **Day 4** | **Luke 23:32–43, The repentant thief** |

# *Session 4*

# FATHER, FORGIVE THEM

## *Aim*

To see the cross more clearly as a focus for forgiveness.

## *Way in*

Do you find it easier to forgive or to receive forgiveness? Discuss this for a few minutes with another member of the group.

### PREPARING

Allow time to pray together about the situations you have just discussed or about anything else individuals may wish to bring before God.

### Songs to sing

'There is a green hill far away', SOF 542, MP 674, LP 204.
'When I survey the wondrous cross', SOF 596, MP 755,
    LP 221(i).
'Bless the Lord, O my soul', SOF 47, MP 56, LP 14.
'Thank you for the cross', SOF 522, MP 632.
'His hands were pierced', MP 232.
'Praise you, Lord', SOF 472, MP 565.
'God forgave my sins', SOF 129, MP 181.
'Lead us, heavenly Father, lead us', SOF 321, MP 400.
'Meekness and majesty', SOF 390, LP 138.

### Music to listen to

Handel: 'Behold, the Lamb of God', from *Messiah*.
Enya: 'Angeles', from *Shepherd Moons*.

# Bible

## Luke 23:32–43

*32 Two others also, who were criminals, were led away to be put to death with him. 33 When they came to the place that is called The Skull, they crucified Jesus there with the criminals, one on his right and one on his left. 34 Then Jesus said, 'Father, forgive them; for they do not know what they are doing.' And they cast lots to divide his clothing. 35 And the people stood by, watching; but the leaders scoffed at him, saying, 'He saved others; let him save himself if he is the Messiah of God, his chosen one!' 36 The soldiers also mocked him, coming up and offering him sour wine, 37 and saying, 'If you are the King of the Jews, save yourself!' 38 There was also an inscription over him, 'This is the King of the Jews.'*

*39 One of the criminals who were hanged there kept deriding him and saying, 'Are you not the Messiah? Save yourself and us!' 40 But the other rebuked him, saying, 'Do you not fear God, since you are under the same sentence of condemnation? 41 And we indeed have been condemned justly, for we are getting what we deserve for our deeds, but this man has done nothing wrong.' 42 Then he said, 'Jesus, remember me when you come into your kingdom.' 43 He replied, 'Truly I tell you, today you will be with me in Paradise.'*

Jesus lived out a life of perfect love (Matt 5:43–48), then showed love in action by his death on the cross. Rather than hating those who had crucified him and those who came to sneer and to mock, he offered up a prayer of forgiveness for them (Luke 23:34).

He frequently spoke of forgiveness when confronted with someone in need of healing; so it was with the paralysed man we are told about in Luke 5:17–25. Just as the body needs healing from disease, so the spirit needs healing through forgiveness of sins. But first we have to admit this need. One of the thieves crucified with Jesus realised this, and he repented by admitting his guilt. Jesus responded by opening for him the gate to paradise.

# *Meditation*

## WHAT IS ONE AMONG SO MANY?

Why do they always choose the hottest days
for this sort of thing?
Getting into the square in front of the Governor's house
was bad enough,
then having to get out here,
you're exhausted before you start.

It's a strange place, Golgotha.
It's as if those who've died here
have left some of their agony behind for you to feel.
When they get started,
and the swearing and screaming begins,
it suddenly goes cold,
even when the sun's beating down on you.

There are three of them today,
two yelling and one who looks as though he's already dead.
He said something about forgiving them,
said they didn't know what they were doing,
but they still banged in the nails.

I couldn't have done it,
but if they say they'll crucify you if you don't, you do it!
It's made me think, seeing this one.
Was he forgiving me for watching?
Am I wrong to be here?
Am I part of it all?
What am I doing here?
It's colder today already, and darker –
it should be hotter and brighter.
Usually I stay to the end, but this death's not right.
I'm going home.

## FOR DISCUSSION / REFLECTION

Are there sometimes obstacles in the way of repentance and for-giveness, of which we need to be aware? For example, the call for justice can sometimes cloak a desire for revenge. And some may see forgiveness as weakness.

Are we sometimes afraid to admit our need for forgiveness?

## Life

Most of us have issues which are unresolved and which require us to be forgiving or repentant. Use this exercise to begin the process of bringing one or two such situations into focus (1 John 1:8–9).

Sometimes, like the repentant thief, we need the impetus to acknowledge where we stand. In a moment or two of quietness, let the Holy Spirit guide you as you go through the following questions.

*What remains unrepented?*

*What remains unforgiven?*

*To whom do I need to speak?*

*What do I need to say?*

## Response

As a group, share one thing each that you have discovered during the Life section.

**PRAYER**

Use this time as an opportunity to share anything that has been particularly significant for you during the session, and to pray about it together. It may be appropriate to suggest that people pray for forgiveness for themselves or offer forgiveness in prayer to others.

Further reflection on the theme for this session will be aided by using the readings for the week and the pattern of prayer outlined on pages 18–19. You may wish to do these, along with the words of praise and the meditation, as a group, or individually throughout the week.

**PRAISE**

**Leader:** Lord, do not rebuke me in your anger.

**All:** Be merciful to me, O Lord.

**Leader:** Do not discipline me in your wrath.

**All:** Be merciful to me, O Lord.

**Leader:** Save me because of your unfailing love.

**All:** Turn, O Lord, and deliver me.

**Leader:** The Lord has heard my cry for mercy; the Lord accepts
my prayer.

*(Based on Psalm 6)*

## Meditation

### FATHER, FORGIVE

I want justice,
we want compensation,
he should be made to pay,
they are liable for damages.

The government must do something,
I know my rights,
we will be heard,
he is entitled,
they are the majority.

The people can't be wrong.
What is the truth?
Who will throw the first stone?
Who has the right?
Who will decide?

Am I strong enough not to seek payment?
Am I sure enough about who I am not to demand my rights?
Does the certainty I hear from the majority make me unsure?
Is the truth clear enough to make me drop the stone and forgive?

# Readings for the week

## 4 Father, forgive them

| Reflection | Day 5 | Luke 15:11–32, The lost son |
| | Day 6 | Acts 7:36–53, God's plan |
| | Day 7 | 2 Corinthians 2:5–11, Forgiveness in practice |

## 5 Praying for others

| Preparation | Day 1 | Job 42:7–10, Job prays |
| | Day 2 | Jeremiah 42:1–12, Jeremiah prays |
| | Day 3 | Luke 18:1–8, Persist in prayer |
| **Meeting** | **Day 4** | **John 19:16b–27, Mary and John** |

## Session 5
# PRAYING FOR OTHERS

## Aim
To understand more about how to pray for others even when things are difficult for us.

## Way in
Are you able to recall a time when, despite personal difficulties, you or someone else was able to pray for or support others? What did you learn from the experience?

### PREPARING
Allow time to pray together, focusing particularly on individuals you know who are facing difficulty at this time.

### Songs to sing
'The Servant King', SOF 120, MP 162, LP 40.
'Make me a channel of your peace', SOF 381, MP 456, LP 124.
'Blest be the tie', SOF 49, MP 60.
'For the beauty of the earth', SOF 112, MP 152.
'Father, I place into your hands', SOF 97, MP 133.
'Jesus, stand among us', SOF 303, MP 381.
'Brother, let me be your servant', SOF 54.
'Lord, keep my heart tender', SOF 359.
'I am weak, but thou art strong', MP 263.

### Music to listen to
Handel: 'How beautiful are the feet', from *Messiah*.
Adiemus: 'Amaté Adea', from *Songs of Sanctuary*.

# Bible

### John 19:16b–27

*So they took Jesus; 17 and carrying the cross by himself, he went out to what is called The Place of the Skull, which in Hebrew is called Golgotha. 18 There they crucified him, and with him two others, one on either side, with Jesus between them. 19 Pilate also had an inscription written and put on the cross. It read, 'Jesus of Nazareth, the King of the Jews.' 20 Many of the Jews read this inscription, because the place where Jesus was crucified was near the city; and it was written in Hebrew, in Latin, and in Greek. 21 Then the chief priests of the Jews said to Pilate, 'Do not write, "The King of the Jews," but, "This man said, I am King of the Jews." 22 Pilate answered, 'What I have written I have written.' 23 When the soldiers had crucified Jesus, they took his clothes and divided them into four parts, one for each soldier. They also took his tunic; now the tunic was seamless, woven in one piece from the top. 24 So they said to one another, 'Let us not tear it, but cast lots for it to see who will get it.' This was to fulfil what the scripture says,*

> *'They divided my clothes among themselves,*
>    *and for my clothing they cast lots.'*

*25 And that is what the soldiers did.*

*Meanwhile, standing near the cross of Jesus were his mother, and his mother's sister, Mary the wife of Clopas, and Mary Magdalene. 26 When Jesus saw his mother and the disciple whom he loved standing beside her, he said to his mother, 'Woman, here is your son.' 27 Then he said to the disciple, 'Here is your mother.' And from that hour the disciple took her into his own home.*

After praying for others to be forgiven, Jesus looked down from the cross and saw his mother and John the beloved disciple. With his death, Mary would need someone to look after her (John 7:5, Jesus knew that his brothers and sisters did not believe in him, whereas Mary did). Through what he said, Jesus gave John the benefit of the wisdom and support Mary could offer, and gave Mary John's care and protection.

Earlier, in Gethsemane, Jesus had asked his disciples to pray for him, but they had fallen asleep when he most needed their support. By asking for prayer as he himself prepared for death, and by praying for others as he died, Jesus reminds us of what it means to show real commitment. By his concern for Mary and John, he shows us how we too can see into the heart of a situation and enable another person to meet a need we cannot fulfil ourselves.

## FOR DISCUSSION / REFLECTION
Sometimes we ourselves are not able to help directly in a difficult situation. We can, nevertheless, assist by involving someone else. Can you think of an instance where this has happened? What was the outcome?

## Life
Spend some time thinking about situations in which you have needed help and when others have asked you for help.

How did you feel, and how did it affect your relationship, when you needed help...

*...but those you asked did not respond?*

*...and someone responded despite their own problems?*

How did it feel, and how did it affect the relationship between you and the person asking, when you were asked for help…

| *…but felt unable to respond? What prevented you?* | *…and you responded, despite your own problems?* |

# Meditation

## THROUGH THE CENTURION'S EYES

How can a man dying like this think about others?
How can he think about his mother's future
when life is ebbing away from him?
Why worry about a friend like this?

It makes me wonder who will worry about me
when I can soldier on no longer.
Who will care about me?
Who will worry about my future?
I know there's a pension,
but who will care like this man cares?
I've got friends in the army now,
but what about when all that ends?
With no army to keep us together, what then?
Will anyone care?
This man's got friends prepared to wait,
to stay with him in a place like this.

Why do I feel this Jesus is speaking to me,
that he's saying things far more important
than any I've heard before?
Why do I think his words have a meaning
which goes far beyond the here and now?
As they nailed him down, I thought,
'What a waste of a young life.'
Now he's about to die, and I see his friends,
I know there is no waste – he's too serene for that.
But what about me?
What does he see when he looks at me?
What would I see if I looked through his eyes?

What could this mother of his teach me?
What could this friend show me?
He loves them, they love him.
Who loves me?

## Response

As a group, share one thing each that you have discovered during the Life section.

**PRAYER**

Use this time as an opportunity to tell others in the group anything that has been particularly significant for you during the session, and pray about it together.

Further reflection on the theme for this session will be aided by using the readings for the week and the pattern of prayer outlined on pages 18–19. You may wish to do these, along with the words of praise and the meditation, as a group, or individually throughout the week.

**PRAISE**

**Leader:** When I am afraid, O God…
**All:** I will trust you.
**Leader:** God, whose word I praise…
**All:** I will trust you.
**Leader:** What can mortal man do to me?
**All:** In God I trust: I will not be afraid.
**Leader:** May I walk before God in the light of life.

*(Based on Psalm 56)*

## Readings for the week

**5 Praying for others**

| Reflection | Day 5 | Exodus 8:20–32, Pharaoh asks for prayer |
| | Day 6 | Colossians 1:3–13, Unceasing prayer |
| | Day 7 | Jude 17–24, Pray in the Holy Spirit |

## 6 The empty cross

| Preparation | Day 1 | Philippians 3:12–21, Pressing on |
|---|---|---|
| | Day 2 | 1 Corinthians 1:18–31, Wisdom of the cross |
| | Day 3 | Galatians 6:1–10, Sharing good things |
| **Meeting** | **Day 4** | **Luke 24:13–35, The road to Emmaus** |

# Session 6
# THE EMPTY CROSS

## Aim
To look at the way in which the cross of Jesus leads to restoration.

## Way in
Discuss with another member of the group a relationship you were involved in or observed, which at one time seemed on the verge of dissolving but which has since been healed or restored.

### PREPARING
Spend time praying together, perhaps giving thanks for the relationships you have just been talking about, or about anything else individuals may wish to bring before God.

### Songs to sing
'In the tomb so cold', SOF 245, MP 340, LP 132.
'How great thou art', SOF 425, MP 506.
'I know that my Redeemer lives', MP 278.
'At your feet we fall', SOF 34, MP 45, LP 10.
'All heaven declares', SOF 10, MP 14.
'All hail King Jesus', SOF 7, MP 11.
'All hail the power of Jesus' name', SOF 9, MP 13 .
'Thine be the glory', SOF 551, MP 689, LP 233.
'Abide with me', SOF 2, MP 4.

### Music to listen to
Handel: 'I know that my Redeemer liveth', from *Messiah*.
Paul McCartney: 'Celebration', from *Standing Stone*.

# Bible

## Luke 24:13–35

[13] Now on that same day two of them were going to a village called Emmaus, about seven miles from Jerusalem, [14] and talking with each other about these things that had happened. [15] While they were talking and discussing, Jesus himself came near and went with them, [16] but their eyes were kept from recognising him. [17] And he said to them, 'What are you discussing with each other as you walk along?' They stood still, looking sad. [18] Then one of them, whose name was Cleopas, answered him, 'Are you the only stranger in Jerusalem who does not know the things that have taken place there in these days?' [19] He asked them, 'What things?' They replied, 'The things about Jesus of Nazareth, who was a prophet mighty in deed and word before God and all the people, [20] and how our chief priests and leaders handed him over to be condemned to death and crucified him. [21] But we had hoped that he was the one to redeem Israel. Yes, and besides all this, it is now the third day since these things took place. [22] Moreover, some women of our group astounded us. They were at the tomb early this morning, [23] and when they did not find his body there, they came back and told us that they had indeed seen a vision of angels who said that he was alive. [24] Some of those who were with us went to the tomb and found it just as the women had said; but they did not see him.' [25] Then he said to them, 'Oh, how foolish you are, and how slow of heart to believe all that the prophets have declared! [26] Was it not necessary that the Messiah should suffer these things and then enter into glory?' [27] Then beginning with Moses and all the prophets, he interpreted to them the things about himself in all the scriptures.

[28] As they came near the village to which they were going, he walked ahead as if he were going on. [29] But they urged him strongly, saying, 'Stay with us, because it is almost evening and the day is now nearly over.' So he went in to stay with them. [30] When he was at the table with them, he took bread, blessed and broke it, and gave it to them. [31] Then their eyes were opened, and they recognised him; and he vanished from their sight. [32] They said to

*each other, 'Were not our hearts burning within us while he was talking to us on the road, while he was opening the scriptures to us?' 33 That same hour they got up and returned to Jerusalem; and they found the eleven and their companions gathered together. 34 They were saying, 'The Lord has risen indeed, and he has appeared to Simon!' 35 Then they told what had happened on the road, and how he had been made known to them in the breaking of the bread.*

For his disciples and supporters, the immediate result of Jesus' arrest and crucifixion was guilt, anger, disillusionment and despondency.

- Simon Peter had denied Jesus three times (John 18:15–17, 25–27), having said he would lay down his life for him (13:37). He would have felt wretched.

- The disciples, collectively, fled Gethsemane (Mark 14:50) and scattered. They had given up much to join Jesus and had come to believe in him. Now it looked as though that belief was ill-founded. They would have felt guilty and disillusioned.

- Those whom Jesus had healed – for example, the sinful woman to whom Jesus had given self-esteem and a new start in life when she anointed him and received his forgiveness (Luke 7:36–50) – would have been angry that he was so unjustly killed.

- Those on the edge of the committed group, who had seen in Jesus new hope for a fresh approach to life – 'We had hoped that he was the one to redeem Israel' (Luke 24:21) – would have been despondent.

We who know that Jesus rose after three days may find their dis-illusionment odd, but at the time the situation was not at all clear and the future looked very dark.

## FOR DISCUSSION / REFLECTION

Can you recall a situation which at one time seemed very bleak but which, looking back, became much brighter? What brought about the change? Are things easier to understand looking at them now?

## Life

Jesus restored the disciples (John 20:19–23; 21:15–19). He appeared especially for Thomas who had doubts (John 20:24–29), and he encouraged those who were despondent (Luke 24:13–31). Sometimes it was clear at once who he was, but on the road to Emmaus and by the Sea of Tiberius (John 21:4) Jesus was not immediately recognised.

## RESTORATION

Are there situations on which you look back, where the presence of Jesus was not at all clear until something particular happened to reveal him to you?

| The situation | How Jesus was discovered |
| --- | --- |
|  |  |

Are there any painful situations in which you are involved, or which you are aware of at present, where Jesus needs to be invited in to restore harmony or well-being?

*The situation*                    *What Jesus is invited to do*

## Response

Share one thing you have discovered during the Life section with others in the group.

**PRAYER**

Use this time as an opportunity to tell others in the group of anything that has been particularly significant for you during all six sessions, and pray about them together. Pray especially for the restoration of relationships.

Further reflection on the theme for this session will be aided by using the readings for the week and the pattern of prayer on pages 18–19. You may wish to do these, along with the words of praise and the meditation as a group, or individually throughout the week.

**PRAISE**

**Leader:** You lifted me out of the depths.
**All:** You healed me.
**Leader:** O Lord, my God, I called to you for help.
**All:** You healed me.
**Leader:** You turned my wailing into dancing.
**All:** I will exalt you, O Lord.
**Leader:** Sing to the Lord, praise his holy name.

*(Based on Psalm 30)*

## Meditation

### RESTORATION

It seemed so easy to go to Emmaus.
Just leave Jerusalem, leave the disciples,
leave the turmoil, leave the confusion.
Much safer out of the way.

Let's face it, we thought it was all over.
Jesus was dead and the eleven were all at sea.
No leader, no one knew what to do next.
Why stay around, adding to the gloom?

Then we met this man on the road,
rather, he joined us.
One minute we were alone,
the next he was with us.

He was a bit odd,
didn't know much about what had been going on,
but what a gift for explaining things.
It was like seeing it all through new eyes.
Suddenly, it all seemed so understandable –
death as a way to new life,
the grave as a place of victory.
He showed us Jesus was not defeated,
how he had overcome his enemies
and would rise on the third day.

Wait a minute, that's today…

When we persuade this man to join us for supper,
he offers thanks over the bread,
and suddenly we realise only one person does it like that.
Jesus.

It's all so clear now,
but it won't make the future any easier.
People won't want to believe us,
but the tomb is empty.
Jesus is alive, restored,
and so are we.
Now all things are possible in his name.

# Readings for the week

## 6 The empty cross

| Reflection | Day 5 | Hebrews 12:1–13, Discipline and hardship |
|---|---|---|
| | Day 6 | 1 Corinthians 2:6–16, Wisdom and the Spirit |
| | Day 7 | Colossians 1:15–23, The supremacy of Christ |

# Available from Scripture Union

### 'I am...': Six studies in John's Gospel for groups
*Tony Kidd*
1 85999 176 9, £3.99
A six-week course which gives a deeper understanding of the claims Jesus made about himself in John's Gospel, exploring their significance for us as Christians, individually and as part of his body, the church.

### The Small-Group Leader: A manual to develop vital small groups
*John Mallison*
1 85999 158 0, £7.99
This valuable book provides insights into the dynamics of groups, along with practical advice on the kind of effective leadership that will keep them alive. Includes study guides.
'Its comprehensiveness means no church should be without one' *(New Christian Herald)*.

### Sunday, Monday: Faith in the world
A six-session course for groups which looks at how to carry your Sunday faith into your life on Monday and throughout the week. The resources book gives practical ideas for group meetings and suggestions for further action.

Resources book (for leaders) 0 86201 987 7, £7.99
Group member's book 0 86201 986 9, £2.50

**Spiritual Encounter Guides**
*Stephen and Jacalyn Eyre*
£3.50 each
A fresh approach to personal devotion for new or long-time Christians. The aim of these Bible studies is to help readers find intimacy with God. Each book contains one month's Bible reading material. Titles include:

**Abiding in Christ's Love**, 1 85999 021 5
**Sinking your Roots in Christ**, 1 85999 022 3
**Sitting at the Feet of Jesus**, 1 85999 020 7
**Waiting on the Lord**, 1 85999 019 3

All these products are available from your local Christian bookshop, or from **SU Mail Order, PO Box 764, Oxford, OX4 5FJ; tel (01865) 716880, fax (01865) 715152**. Please add £0.75 postage and packaging for the first book, and £0.50 for subsequent books, up to a maximum of £2.75.

For a complete catalogue of resources from Scripture Union, please contact **SU Sales and Promotions, 207-209 Queensway, Bletchley, Milton Keynes, MK2 2EB; tel (01908) 856000, fax (01908) 856111**.